The poems in Sunni Wilkinson's *The Marriage of the Moon and the Field* show us history, affection, private struggle, and the common life with a kind of grave, irony-tinged happiness that is rare in the poetry of our time. Her poems turn away from complaint, as though she had set out to reveal instead the domestic life of intelligence in all its color, warmth, and depth. This is a very fine debut volume, worth treasuring; and more are sure to follow.
—**Christopher Howell**

Sunni Brown Wilkinson's poems sustain a compelling tension between the macro and micro worlds. Scientific facts of the physical realm collide with intimate interiorities. She turns a steely eye and a tender heart toward the experience of living fully in the rush of the NOW and the flickering echoes of what came before. These are lushly rendered poems to savor and/or to devour.
—**Nance Van Winckel**

The Marriage of the Moon and the Field

Sunni
Brown
Wilkinson

Black
Lawrence
Press

www.blacklawrence.com

Executive Editor: Diane Goettel
Cover and Book Design: Amy Freels
Cover Art: "Pomegranate Tree" by Kristin Carver

Copyright © Sunni Brown Wilkinson 2019
ISBN: 978-1-62557-004-8

Published 2019 by Black Lawrence Press.
Printed in the United States.

For Sean, Cael, Beck and Cooper

And for Jude, a hand on the other side

Contents

There are, it may be, so many kinds of voices in the world,
and none of them is without signification.
    1 Corinthians 14:10

This world is the other world.
    Robert Hass, *Twentieth Century Pleasures*

I.

Translation

To speak to Moses, God
put a stone in his mouth, put on

a sackcloth of verbs (*want*, *need*),
cleared his throat. Cried out.

The same way the meadowlark
uses five notes to call us

back to the burgeoning world,
or the burkwood

near the hospital doors
whispers of my father, the unbearable

softness of his face and the bright up–
rightness of his body: a feeble house

for what will live forever.
The same way the ghost enters—

humbly—the brittle hardware
of our bodies, or hidden fires hum

in all the wires of the house,
shuttling what we live by. It's

how translation works,
conception. Not St. Elmo's Fire

but a light bulb. That's why we kiss
with cracked and speechless mouths,

why the captured lark is silent.
That's why the bush burned.

Smoke Signals

It starts like this: evening, a boy in a dorm room
calls home. He's casual, but with each joke
he pulls the looping phone cord closer,
trying to shorten the distance

between himself and the old life.
On the other end, his mother in her tasteful
makeup and cream–colored suburban home

knows it
the way she knows there's a God
and asks him what's wrong.

It's an old AT & T ad, and the music starts.
When the people you love come through
loud and clear a man says,
and you want to cry. You want to sleep

inside that moment and believe,
as Machado says,
that we are good in the good
sense of the word. *Reach out and touch*

someone. My father called home the night
he shipped out for Vietnam. He'd signed up
to camp and fight and sleep
under the stars, but he couldn't say that
to his mother. Instead, he said

nothing. She traded *We love you*
for *Okay*. Fourteen months in the jungle
of regret. We all feel bad. We're all heartsick

sometimes: strangers in the architecture
and burning incense at the temples,
the names of ancestors in calligraphies of smoke
we can't read.

Aunt Peggy shipped my father cigarettes,
though she thought they were bad
for his health. He smoked them at sunrise
before the shooting started,

sent the smoke up like a signal
that was neither loud nor clear.

My Son Says He Has an Owl Inside of Him,

soft with large, sad eyes.
      The snow has not stopped falling
all morning, and I am pregnant,
and the baby is soft and has eyes
we can't see.

In the garden,
      white slowly smothers
the flowers, lights lining the walk,
the goose–necked gas meter ugly
in its protrusion.
                  Gone.
What falls now
      remakes the world.

Inside me an orchid
      unwraps itself.
In the exam room,
on the black and white screen,

particles swirl around the child.
      What will he find when he comes?
      Was it worth the work of making

himself?
Loose matter gathers
around and inside him—
      a snow globe settling.
Even when the doctor turns off

the screen, prints the images, something
falls into place,

       something crouches, unwinds, prepares

to fly. All day I wonder
    if the world is enough.

Pieces of light fall
endlessly.

The owls inside us open their wide eyes.

Girls of the Underworld

The beginning of the names
are strange, but the endings
the same. That long *e* stretching
out, giggling or squealing.
Like the string on the end of a kite
or the mean little tail of a bright–eyed
shrew.
       Persephone, Eurydice.

~~~~

These are the wages of beauty:
to be both captivating
      and captive.

They took to wearing black
to blend in. But their faces
      were the flame
on a lit match, their hair the smoke
that gave everything away.

~~~~

One had a good mother.
That helped. She tried to fish the girl out
first, with a long pole,
but the god there found it, broke it over
his knee. She buried a message

deep in the earth saying,
   Eat, and you stay.

That night in the god's dreams, the girl
   was a peach. In her dreams,

he was a pomegranate.

~~~~

She wasn't alone.
Another girl showed up
with a snake bite
  and a husband
who could sing
just like Dylan, though his tux
was tattered after months
  of searching
and he wasn't good
with rules. He couldn't
  carry her out
like he wanted, like the day
they got married and she danced
in the meadow and the little house
waited in the oaks. Instead,
he had to walk in front
  like a criminal,
his one look back
a slamming door.

~~~~

The first girl awoke
         to hunger.   The god in the doorway
was waiting.

Approaching the Threshold

"Dr. Alejandro Hernández Cárdenas took a scorched-
looking, decomposed head and five stiff, bloated hands
and gently submerged them in his secret solution. 'After
they soak for three days,' he said, 'any scars, lesions or
birthmarks the victim might have had will reappear...'
His technique, normally applied to full bodies, can restore
murder and identity clues."

"Doctor's Bath for Corpses Reinvigorates Cold Cases."
The New York Times. Tuesday, October 15, 2012.

1.
He started with Gerber jars
filled with cloudy fluid

and teeth. Now a mummified
head waits on a table

while in a tub
whole bodies soak, Jacuzzi–like.

The women of Juarez
are salvaged like junkyard parts

from the desert. (Parts
they never found—nipples,

some toes, fingers severed
at the knuckle.)

They're brought here in bags,
submerged

until they talk: birthmarks
blotchy as stains

bleeding back,
highways of the palm

resurfacing. Mothers and lovers
come to read them

like fortunes. Message
in a body, a door

unlocking.

2.
My six–year–old reads of monsters
and mythology: sea beast curls
over ship sailing into blue
and a woman with snakes for hair
(how does she comb it?) kisses gorgons, and a girl
trapped in the underworld spins. Eats pomegranates.
Chews her nails. Was it hard
to get out,
even when it was time? Did she climb
underground volcanoes, swim up
the whole ocean, dodge the sea beast and pull
herself fingernail by shoulder onto shore?
Or was there a door?

3.
When planes go down over the ocean
and people search for the black box

that sings *ping   ping   ping*
like a submarine,
who is searching
for the door to the room
the lost entered
like a party
they'd always heard—
pulsing—
and were finally let in?

4.
On the stereo, he plays ballads, love songs,
woos and comforts dead women in a den

of puce liquids and glycerin. *I take many girls
to bed,* he jokes, holding their bodies at night, *but not*

the way you think. He carries them to the bath
the way a man carries his bride

over the threshold. Slowly the women return
to a state of origin, like Pangaea

on a screen in fourth grade geography,
the parts moving back into place.

5.
On our tour of Lake Union,
in a bus that turns into a boat,

we watch the rows of floating
houses sway a little. I wonder

if the doors swell, if stepping
from boat to doorstep

is tricky. Or do you leap?
We stop for photos

in front of a yellow house
owned by a TV star.

He hosts a gameshow the old people
at my oma's rest home

watched. They would drift
forward in their wheelchairs,

swollen and tired, staring
at the red curtain,

waiting for that moment
when all the prizes are unveiled.

6.
My son reads *Choose Your Own Adventure*.
In one called *Mystery*
Of the Maya, someone kidnaps a girl,

hides her in a temple
of ruins. You have to find
her. You have to save her

from the men in masks. Every moment
counts. Every turn
a different door.

7.

In Juarez, a man lifts pieces   of a woman
          from the bathtub   brings her
back   to the night   it happened:

she waited   for the green bus
          to take her
to work in *maquiladora.*
          All around her   women
thin frames   long dark hair   just like her—
          a hall of mirrors.

The green bus   the edge of night
          and all the women
              stepping on.

Two Sides of the Same

Oglala—the sound of it like a punch to the gut
then a song. Crazy Horse was thirty–six
when he died. When he opened
his eyes on the other side, I want to believe
he was hungry again, the old meddling
ache lifting him up, the fruit of the dark
and the light so much like water.

We rise from a sleep like water. In the kitchen,
the fruit flies are still there, though I threw out
the fruit two days ago. At breakfast
they sail past our faces. They've camped
in the vase of roses to say *We have infinite houses.*
We're not going away.

Sioux. Say it. The *oo* curving your lips
in amazement. In the Moon of Making Fat
the elderberries swelled and the colts ate a world
of grass. When the moon rose, the milk of it spilled
onto this world's fields and the next world's
pines. Crazy Horse could see both
without closing his eyes.

In the new basement, I'm confused:
the pull chain changed to a switch and hallways
where there used to be doors. I once walked
through walls. Only the light is the same.
When the white dust settles
from the sheetrock and I walk in my socks

to the storage for another box of cereal,
ghost prints follow me back. They hang
around for days. They're all over
the house, like evidence of guests
we live with and don't see.

Nesting Dolls

The biggest one carries all that weight
inside her it's a wonder

she doesn't fall over.
Pull apart her two halves and out

comes another, rouged and ready
to open again. Quiet, and you can hear them

breathe, a tiny ocean
sound in each. Just now a thump

under my ribs says *No more room*
in this borrowed house. Like cells slowly dividing,

we make our peace by letting go.
It's almost time. We're verses

with space in between
for our own small hallelujah. *Selah,*

the Hebrew word that marks a rest
after each Psalm. I want to say *Selah* in between

each house on my block, all the sleepers
in soft places. When the wind tore

at our house and I was afraid
the big pine would fall,

we all slept in the front room,
nothing but our breath, covers rising

and falling, a stone–light
through the blinds,

two children and their parents
dreaming. Deeper inside, the unborn

tapped, and the train whistle cried out—
my son says, *like someone calling your name.*

St. Francis of Assisi Church, Vienna

This church is a man with dirt in his toes and rosy cheeks.
A man who whistles, carries a satchel with a few scraps
of food, waves to strangers. And here in the Mexican Quarter,
the locals call him Jubilee, the happiest of saints. We have sailed

through beer and wine and castle country and have come
to something new: the Danube dark and still,
the Sturgeon moon rising over a street lamp,
and a picnic table where two men and two women in burkas

drink tea. In a park marked by a chain link fence,
their children play. We have stepped out of a postcard
and into the real: a family, a moment with the day's
last tea and bread. St Francis is tired and snores in the dark,

and the black robes of the Syrian women sweep the ground
around him. We breathe in the evening air, as human
as we'll ever be. Parents lift small cups to their faces,
children play. From a bench, my husband and I watch.

Back home their country is smoke and rubble. Ours is strip malls,
vending machines, the toxic light of the evening news
telling us how to feel. In the story, all the creatures of the earth
come to St. Francis. The birds sing on his shoulders

and the rabbits gather at the foot of his robe. He is cloaked
in the gold of their animal love. Tonight even the sturgeon
comes, that primitive fish swimming in the clouds.
As we stand up to go, one of the men reaches out,

waves us over with the cup in his hand. *Come*, he says,
please, and motions toward the table where his wife rises
to meet us and puts out her small hand
over the fence. Her face is a moon shrouded in dusk,

and her son is the size of our youngest. The man is learning
German, comes from Damascus. Two years in this
country, studying, *This country good to us.* Country of saints
and Ave Maria, of city parks green under the moonlight,

of bread and pastries and paintings in domed buildings.
St. Francis is the moth beating his heart against the bulb
of the street lamp, the red-roofed church, the shadowed grass
where we step toward strangers, hold out our hands.

How His Fingers Trembled

We saw him once, crossing the street
to the Island Market, a short man
with a body like tinder, and my father said
that was the nervous boy from high school
who wore his face in his hands and had one
friend, an easy-going athlete, and the two
stayed close even after, the one under the wing
of the other.

They went bow hunting once
among trees, and the light
pushed away and broke
into fragments. Or was it dark
and the brushing against bark,
those seams of a forest that never end?
And all the while the crackle and breath
of trees and their own bodies
moving.

What is tenderness
if not the finger on the arrow? What is grief
if not the quivering gone wrong? The arrow sailed
past the ghost of some bright animal
and into the heart of his friend.
You know the story, surely,
how he brought his body
to the truck and drove to tell
his friend's pregnant wife what he'd done.
How he stayed in his room for months
and no one knew how to come close
or break the tether of his ache. How

years later he asked my mother
on a date in winter, washed his car the day
before, and all the locks froze. How he stood
on the curb next to her, under falling snow,
lighting matches, setting the flame
carefully
against the keyhole.

At Last the Light in the Trees Wavers

and moves on like an old woman
turning away

from the mirror. Everything dims.
Now the lamp

is master. November,
and the rake face–

down in a pile of leaves
is like a kid playing dead,

the stick of his back staying
perfectly still.

And at night in our bed
the bird of me returns

to the tree of you.
All we've shed: leaves

and feathers on the floor.
The dark and your limbs

draw me in.
I'll sing now

in my little house of bones.

The Body Carries Its Own Light

1.
Dark horses, Mary. Dark shoulders in the dusk of your long hair.
Blue dusk where I sit with you, brushing your hair the color

of the wood your father split in Chiapas where he farmed,
was it coffee? Your mother one of many wives there. Black horses

in the darkness that covered the farm where your mother found you
slumped and breathless. The other wives crying, pushing

the children out of the way of the doctor who came
on foot, having tended to the horses, their long hair

so much like yours, Mary, damp with sweat and clinging
to your tiny face, fair for Mexican and now blue, now gray.

The walnuts you were eating scattered on the table in disarray. This is
before Cecy. This is when the darkness took over everything

and left you, for the first time, alone. The wives clinging to each other
and pale. Your mother's face a little cloud. Your beautiful mother.

The one who came at dusk so the ceremony would be brief
like the wedding night itself, like the moments

that bloomed between them when the smell of wood was not fetid
yet, though the smell of coffee never was. Where was your father

with the fields too shadowed for harvest or planting?
In the stables, one mare lay back wearily and the strange sac

between her legs,
torn and white, once encasing her foal,

lay still. Still and white and shining. No more breathing
inside it. No more breathing.

Where did you go then, Mary?

2.
Today at the breakfast table, Cecy coos to you, teases and coos
traviesa, flaca, que quieres, mi amor? Cecy who came here

under a tarp in a truck, who crossed parts of the desert
alone, who will never go back. She feeds you through a tube

and you blink to say thank you. She washes your legs and arms,
your whole body long for eight and stiff. Cecy

rubs your muscles to keep them
from knotting, to keep them strong for the day

she believes you will walk through the gates of Paradise
before us all, not contrite

but like a terrible horse, trampling the last embers of the dark
with your tiny hooves.

3.

In a dream of the possible, the mare waits, panting. The foal inside her
trembles. Your father rises out of the dark of a new woman and walks

to where you sit at a table eating walnuts alone,
your small legs swinging. He has come slowly, full of bitter coffee

and the feast of the body of a new bride. He has come to find you,
drawn as if by the darkness itself that breaks over him like waves,

driving him toward the marriage of the moon and the field,
toward the mare, now opening her body for the terrible letting-go,

toward you, Mary,
little bride of your own body.

II.

Tiger, Hyena Still at Large

In the aftermath of the flood
that freed the zoo animals
in a city as big as Detroit
on the other side of the world,
the gates clattered and the mud
bloomed. Men led a tranquilized hippo
down the street and reached
for monkeys in front yard trees
like college buddies
rounding up the gang
when everyone's had one
too many. When the prophets cry
The Lord is coming! I see the hippo
and the men with their hands
on his back
walking out of the waters,
and all the lost
souls floating at the gates of the zoo,
and the keeper's reckoning:
only two

missing, while the pair of shadows
stalking streets at night
or crouching in alleys
for weeks torment the city,
and all that time
the living locked at home, eating
their last bread and the news.

The tiger and hyena
wild with delight: blood
on their lips,
apocalyptic grins.

Kelly O'Brien and the Choirs of Heaven

In our neighborhood, it's always the same.
Lawrences on their paper route every morning
at six, Vigil's dog squatting on a corner
of our lawn. And Kelly O'Brien walks a block to the Conoco
for Coors, morning and noon, unshaven and slow.
July, in pajamas and sandals. December, trench coat
and beanie. The usual brown bag cradled
in one hand. Kelly O'Brien limping
in the heat or the cold, that bag like an infant
he can't wait to love.

Never holding fruit or medicine. Never
at the movies with a friend, never the park
on the bleachers in the middle of a joke, no one
throwing back their heads in laughter. Never Penney's
or Sears, buying slippers and lingerie
for a *lady friend*. Just the single
strip of pavement from his apartment
to the gas station. Vigilant keeper
of appointments.

The one Sunday he came to church (sky blue
suit tight around the arms, wide collar
from the days of disco), he took over
the pulpit at testimony time, stuck out
his gut, hitched up his pants, offered a few
thank yous.
Awkward as hell up there.
        Silence below.

Like a rebel coming home
for a bite to eat: conversation dries up,
everyone stares
at the table, the saucepan burns
the last bit of gravy black.

The chorister cried while she led
the last song, and I want to think he shook
a few hands when the meeting was done.
Kelly O'Brien in the sands of time,
somebody's son, someone's uncle or brother,
dear God, maybe
somebody's father. Kelly O'Brien
in the robes of heaven, our best sermon,
the bread we taste
before our mouths tear it to pieces.

Connie Wolf, the Lady Balloonist from Blue Bell Pennsylvania, Confesses

> "[O]ne of the most noticeable phenomena of balloon flight is the clarity of sounds from below."
> Eric Sloane, *Folklore of American Weather*, 1963

Crossing the Alps about killed me.
I never dared say it, but it's true. In 1962
I was brazen, almost blonde, and I knew
I could do what men say and men do.
It was August, and I was childless,
and the hot air drove me to it.
Those peaks were Alexandria,
and I was Cleopatra to their thrones.

But something in me broke
up there. I missed the smell of bread
and bacon, of garlic turning silky
in the pot. My nose turned to dampness.
I sneezed a lot.

Which is not to say I was lonely
(my best company were
birds) just that I was tempered
in a solid drift of wind
in a basket in a foreign land
to see the world for what it is, but more
than that, to hear it. Not rumors

of laughter but the laugh itself
rising up, *Danke* between neighbors,

crisp closing of a door, the cracked falsetto
of a boy milking cows.

They came to me as sacraments
I ate and ate. It was a new faith:
hearing what I couldn't see
and believing what I only heard.
Villages lifted up their tokens

as I passed. I knew then
all our colloquial and private ways
and knew I'd always known. The way
the old farmer, hearing the storm first
in the chimney
knows the language of the rain.

Gumballs

My grandfather wanted to make millions
on gumballs. This was after the vitamins

in hard white bottles he bought by the case
that were going to make him millions

and just before he sponsored a concert pianist
always on the brink of success

and during his stint in SoCal real estate
when something went sour, and a handful

of years after he married my grandmother
and they lived in Palm Springs: golf course

off the patio, twin Mercedes in the garage.
He bought millions of gumballs, golf ball big

but smooth, brought a box to our house,
said we should sell them to the neighbor kids,

as if we were Wall Street brokers. Instead,
we loaded them in a wagon, dragged them

in slow, humiliated steps around the block.
My grandfather had been a millionaire

but his money was draining and he wanted more.
The way, years before, he'd surprise-kissed

my grandmother, his good friend's wife,
long and full in the kitchen when they were married

to their first loves, a *thank you for visiting*
gone wrong. No one wanted gumballs so the box

stayed full in my brother's closet next to his
smelly high-tops and that bag of weed he hid

from my parents. This was around the time
we fell in love with rock (Zeppelin, U2), caught

lizards in the foothills. We were young
but not small. My uncle said I was *blooming*

and I couldn't look at him for years.
The gumballs collected dust.

Sometimes we rinsed them off, broke their shells
with our teeth and chewed

until our jaws hurt and the gum
slowly hardened like cement

drying and we couldn't open our mouths
except to jerk them suddenly

like that jaw-dropping moment
a strange man sat on our couch

and hugged and kissed our grandma
like a kid getting his fill in a candy store.

Envy

Why so much angst
in the morning? Everything wants attention.
Clock waving its hands
minute by precise minute. Dozens of houseplants
calling *feed me*. Refrigerator's high-pitched
incessant whirring. It must sing its importance.
Well, I know. I've been a slave all day
to ticks and rings and whirs. A woman I know
had a dryer so full of want it burst
into flames, burned the whole house down.
I feel sorry for them: things. How sad
it must be, how frustrating
to know their limits: they are not eternal
or unbearably beautiful, unlike the person
whose hands stroke them every day, saying
I'm here. I'll always be here.
I will live forever.

Mary Cassatt

The young man who flies from New York to Salt Lake to fill in
for a famous pianist (stomach flu) is also a famous pianist. We
are second row at the symphony, and the pianist is skinny,
early 20s, and he plays a song like lanterns crashing.
Something modern. But first he plays Beethoven. We watch
him sway on the piano bench, eyes closed, anchored by his
torso and pointed leather shoes, and I wonder about his
mother. How many hours of practice did she hear? The
Emperor Suite over a screaming pot of tea. Endless staircases
of Chopin while she plucked his clean underwear from the
basket, folded the waistband in half, tucked under the crotch.
And for all the art about Paris or the sea, why not more about
laundry? About children, teaching them to pee like grown-ups:
elbows on their knees, legs swinging while they wait, wait,
wait, afterward the curved pink mark on their bottoms, a
funny frown. Sweet Mary Cassatt, what do I owe you? What
can I give you, who are both hands and mirror? In *The Bath* the
beautifully plain mother washes the feet of her daughter. They
gaze downward like suburban saints. Quiet, ceremonial. The
heart is harnessed in a thimble and every day it's the morning
of creation. My son on an evening walk at four years old says
the moon looks like a floating egg mama I love living on earth.

Crawley

They found it at Moon Lake in the fine dark sand near the
stream that runs from the mountains and feeds into the lake.
Our sons dug with beach shovels, little moons of sand on their
bottoms. Then, like a secret a child tells behind a hand, the
turtle was suddenly there—sea blue and plastic—and they
named him Crawley because that's what turtles do. He goes
with us now in the car, to all the lakes we know. Sometimes he
rests in the garden. For weeks my son asks everyone we meet if
they've been to Moon Lake. No one has. All this nonsense
about the world being small.

Little Owl in a Dark Room

singing whoo whoo, and the creaks
of the old crib as he lifts

himself up. Summer in the covers
and fall around the house.

Stillness. Now whoo whoo
and ba ba ba. In the oldest language

he lifts the morning
over our heads. The ceiling

tilts as I rise. Cold wood like a river
under my feet.

Fall in a Triptych

1.

The leaves' infectious lecture about dying
is spreading wild across town.
On my morning run, they meddle

in the garbage of the gutter,
the metal flash of a wrapper
next to their sighs,

and in between their papery skins
the near answers we hear. What if what I fear
never leaves me? At three, my son loves dinosaurs

until we visit the museum: panic—
and his hands are frantic birds
tearing at our shirts.

Fear carves
our limits and we stroke them
in the dark hull of ourselves,

letting our fingers drift
over their terrible edges,
So this is the tale I tell my son.

2.

Isaac lived with his father and mother
near a place called Mount Moriah, and here he climbed
as if he were climbing the world
and loved it, for his name meant laughing. He was the breath
in his mother's song, the lifting of his father's
footstep. He was beloved. And one day his father
lifted him skyward
and lay him on an altar.
The world was big above him.
He saw he could not be a bird's
soft body sailing into the light every morning.
He saw the worm, before it entered the bird,
writhing. His father's hands shook
and lingered over him
and the angel showed up in the nick of time.

3.

On the radio
the conversation is money and blood.

In the maple grove it's just blood
but along the hill the aspen are rattling

their gold coins. They could be laughing.
In the growing cold, men seek the bodies

of their wives who cradle
the bodies of their children: light, almost

feathered, smelling faintly of sleep.
I fold myself around my son.

There is nothing that is not
changeable.

Even the ram
became a bright fire.

III.

West Yellowstone

The painted trout over Jacklin's Fly Shop,
Open-mouthed and arched mid-air,

has always been there. He is caught at the end
of an invisible line. He has come

out of evening's waters,
gulping the world as we did at nineteen

in a town crowded with bars and hotels,
Dan and the boys exchanging wooly buggers

for beers, we girls with our hair curled
under Dairy Queen lights.

We left after midnight, stereo blasting
and the Cavalier jammed with knees,

something reckless in our breathing,
until we reached

Firehole River and scaled
the cliffs rimming its edges.

Then Nick would sit on a rock,
shine a flashlight onto the dark

waters churning, and the light—
a pale yellow circle jerking about—

spelled out where to go.
It was an easy thing then.

Twenty years in the turning
of moon to moon. The moss–

speak of the ancients
we can almost hear.

They gather in some soft place
we lean into, closer.

Dan in a *home* now
and Nick teaching Biology

somewhere in the Midwest,
the rest of us parents—

all of us the same: leaping out
into a wavering shaft of light

then swimming,
swimming furiously in the dark.

Quake Lake

Half–buried in water
the aspen stand.
In their old life
on the hill,
fawns groomed
and grazed against
their sides,
dawn like a
grease fire
devoured the wood.
Now

after the trembling
after the spasm,
they rise cold
and exhausted
from the center
of a lake.

A ranger says
the earthquake took
fifty–two lives
but no one
counted these.
Gone

the deer and the leaves.
They are old men
lost, mottled skin,
and no one visiting.

Culinary Arts

It's not so much the steam rising
or raining down the window
behind the jar of olive oil
or the tender potatoes sinking into a sea
of cream, as it is the smell
seeping into my clothes. I feel wise
cooking soup: an old woman
with twigs in my hair
stirring in a few vegetables
from our ragged garden, a crow calling
from the cottage window. Does a golden-haired
child play with thimbles and magic beans
in a corner of the room?
I will not add toadstools and the trouble
they bring. Though maybe I'm a witch:
stew-woman stirring
my maniacal stir, eyeing the children
in their tiny cages, listening to the moans
from their chapped lips.
When the flesh is all gone, the bone-broth
will do.

But today,
in my pink Formica kitchen,
the ubiquitous black pot
in every frame of fact and fiction
looks shrunken on my 1970s
electric range. And the mushrooms
I just added to the wild rice soup

I lifted from a pile
in the produce section at Smith's,
not from the mossy floor
of a forest where the thrush lets fall
its litany of velvety notes.
(And there is nothing wild
about the rice either.)
But tonight, after my husband drifts
into mortal sleep, I will tip-toe
out the back door, onto the wet grass
and dance wildly under the stars,
still smelling of soup, and in my hand
a cracked wooden spoon.

My Possible Pasts

I.

Young girl, Mediterranean

I watched her, gypsy dancer,
my sister seduced by a violin, now
quiet behind the caravan
weaving through the forests of Andalusia
where trees are so dark
we bury ourselves in them.

I am two steps away
from the sleep that turns me gray.
Each nightfall, mother's yellow lanterns
hang in a neat row: faery lights,
she says, trailing
to the end of the earth.

I step up lightly
onto the bridge of night. Always
I am one footfall short of home.
The red hem of my childhood skirt
falls with each year.
A black evening brushes
my father's head, until
he climbs up into it.

II.

Woman, Northern Europe

How strange the planets
in their ringing concentric
songs. I hear their hum
from underneath the snowy
down of my midnight bed. Air
ticks in the machinery of night.

My husband's eye
has grown long with looking
through warped glass at the sky.
The men who gather Thursday mornings
in our tiny parlor speak *discovery*
and brush their boots loose
of the sooty ash of the mine.

My unborn children lost,
my mother far away.
In the longest of summer days
I hear the fir tree seeding,
the reaching of each upright needle.
The planets sing their silence.
Earth is a coin
cast for luck.

III.

Old Man, England

At noon, women at court wander careless
and ornate: peacock feathers waving in the sun.

Tonight, their voices in the bathhouse flutter
above rings of light and rings of water.

My daughter returns home smelling of fish
and lye. Eighteen years, dress cinched

where once loose, she travels outside of herself,
leaving kettle to scorch on the stove.

They say she waits for him by the dock, white
dress blowing: a funnel of fire at sunset. They say

he is a quiet man, netting the restless fish
with his steady hands. I have walked

through the market many mornings,
searching for such a man. Once, I thought

he called to me, but the crowd behind
hurried me on. I turned away.

Once, when she was ten, she mended a hem,
then tore it open again, just to hear the seam tear.

Now, when I ask her where she has been, she turns,
full of a longing I have never known.

Acrobats

On the television, a preacher in a black suit
is talking about *grace*. His face quivers
just before the tears come, and he asks
that I awaken my faith. It is always this way
at two o'clock on channel nine. Sometimes,
hours later, I imitate his piety
for the mirror

and sometimes I think of the homeless man
who crossed the street for my two dollars,
the skittish horses of his eyes
unbearably ashamed.

He said something
about food stamps
being late, an apology
of sorts. I wanted to tell him
something good
but instead I held out the stiff bills
as if I were holding him
at gunpoint. I wanted to say

we were just two acrobats
swinging the same high-rise routine,
tip-toeing it out
for an audience of cars
and traffic lights.

The Spirits Called Legion Speak

"He said unto him, Come out of the man, thou unclean spirit.
And he asked him, What is thy name? And he answered,
saying, My name is Legion: for we are many.
And he besought him much that he would not send them
away out of the country."
Mark 5:8–10

In a place called Gadarenes
we found the man: alone, picking shells
from the beach, the road there
cut off and brambled. Oh, the deep
waiting and the deeper cold,
and finally this shape we could
cast in. We liked the hum
of his blood—a thousand bees
banging—the slits in his palms and the rings
of his eyes. And you know what they say,
location, location...It worked out
for a while, but the hunger got old.
All those wandering years with no feet
of our own and our only mouth
his ragged mouth and our only food
his sobbing. Surely, those pigs will do.
After all, it had been rather crowded,
and the semblance of warmth in the friction
of his lashings never lasted. So what if
we grunt, snouts to the ground, squeal
like little girls? The grass is sweet,
and our hooves on the stones make a musical
mad hammering. From the top of the cliff,
the sky is a highway, and the sea
is the body of God.

The Hidden Honey

"African Tribesmen Can Talk Birds Into Helping Them
Find Honey,"
        The New York Times. July 22, 2016.

In the woods of Mozambique, there is hidden honey
in the trees. Men below with their long, white
teeth and broad lips make a single sound and a little bird

goes hunting, racing to find bees' nests, to smell
again that sweetness. Meanwhile, at the end of my street
the Congolese refugees arrive. They ride their bikes past

the rows of houses, their rainforest replaced by scrub oak
and suburbs, bonobos by common dogs. They yell *Welcome!*
when I arrive with old shoes and kitchen towels. Evenings

at the water park, I hold the youngest in my lap
and slide, and each time he runs up again, shivering
with delight. His uncle says, *15 years in the camp, now here.*

We see his grandfather's red hat around town, crowning
the artless pace of a man taking it in. It's not easy
for the birds—bee stings, the tangled, nearly

unreachable corners of the woods—but the hooked
beak is a weapon even the youngest can use.
The little one leaps from my lap, tries to slide down

alone, his tiny body churning in the water at the bottom
before someone dives in. He was born in a camp,
has traveled farther than any postage stamp

my sons have ever seen. After the men follow
the winged honeyguide and smoke out the trees
and take the honey, scientists say the birds

eat the wax. It's a pact between humans and birds
centuries in the making, each generation
teaching the next. On the news, it's shootings,

rafts in the sea, the chaos that breaks
a hope we've dreamed of, delicate: a stirring inside
the trees, a sweetness so rich it catches at the back of the throat.

Wake

after Henry James

Always a young man in clean boots and a small white
bird churning the sky into ash. He climbs ladders,
the young man,
not towards the bird but a girl
soon to die, and he watches

the coughing, the flashes of eyes
and a long boat moored
under the parapets of Venice. By day,

a face pressed to the glass,
a window opens, and outside a man
with hat in hand and the intricate gardens
shifting their greens. He sighs. She laughs a little.

At night, tiger–faced and hungry,
the costume party reels its usual
plots: deception, the fever of loss.

We are all of us
instinctively tribal. What the labyrinth spells
is not organized chaos
or the map to forgetting
but a blueprint of the wound
we rise every day to cover.

The girl dies. The young man lifts an umbrella
to the falling sky, brushing the spent air
of the bird's flight.
After the wings, the breast opens.

Concertato

Canning tomatoes. Globular reds roiling
and bountiful in the large pot.
The silky skin puckers and tears.
Cooler, in your hands they nearly pulse.
Cut out the green heart.
Outside, finches in the neighbor's maple
haggle over the view singing, *Look, look
how lucky you are.* Old Gene is going,

sits on his porch every day
waving goodbye
to the bright world, even his thin white hair waving.

At the door, a mosquito haphazardly skates on the glass
and behind it
finches spark, fulgurant, striking suddenly
into the trees
like thrown confetti. In the opera on the stereo the lovers
have just met. She opens a window
and he is there, below,
and she is too bright for the modern world.

Bottled, each tomato presses its face
against the glass, curious and childlike,
like a heart thumping in wonder,

like the soft knock at the door. Open it
and there is a dead finch
yellow at the heart and one feather on the glass.

Pick it up. Open your hands and Gene waves hello,
pitches hard, letting an invisible baseball go.
We have lived
in this same neighborhood and never touched.

The wind blows
and suddenly a tree reaches for the door.
The lovers touch. They will not die
in each other's arms but the song
will go like this, *Look
how lucky you are.*

IV.

Passage

Six p.m. closes in on the plane and the noise and the silence
push against each other. The businessman clutches
his cell phone. The conversation we heard—
She gets a million dollars and the kids; I want everything else—

hangs in the air around him. At the back, a baby cries
though its mother has been there
all along: rocking, humming. You are next to me,
and Lake Michigan is below.

High up, in this moving room with strangers,
we are close and you are quiet
and more than ever that man who lifted
my dying friend last summer

into the sunlight and carried her in your arms
down the long beach so she could hear the waves
and the gulls, so she could watch our boys dig
in the sand with shovels the color of crayons,

so she could try on my life in your arms
and sit in the sun next to her mother
and all afternoon remember herself
weightless and beloved

before she is carried
where she was meant to go.
As we are carried now.
A fine evening light washes

over our hands
and the worried baby and the man
who is losing everything and the people
already sleeping.

Childhood at Home

Burkwood against brick, and the tendrils
of the bean plants curl like tiny pigs' tails.

Mother is crying again deep in the house.
The burkwood is a white flower

that blooms in spring and smells
like the bottom of dreams, and inside a room

that pavane endlessly plays.
Father's postal hat on the railing says

he's there comforting her, and outside
the bean plants reach in the dirt and the light

muscles through apertures of cloud
and the clouds are not so much scarves

as horses, all the horses you ever wanted,
riding the sky and calling deep in their throats.

You can ride them into tomorrow, you with the blue
veins that branch through you like bean plants

just under the skin, the ragged white flowers
of your hands against the brick of a house

where a door inside opens and closes
like a throat opens and closes

like a cry that becomes a song
only you hear and understand.

Autobiography With Birds

Willow Park shrouded in a dusk that hushed the monkeys. I heard
the peacocks
shuffle their wild feathers, their tiny fires of noise like flamenco's
castanets.

Our family's pet parrot learned to cry like my brother Riley.
Even when Riley was gone, we heard him crying all through the
house.

Haircuts on the back porch and towels around our shoulders. Ears
glistening.
One month later: robin's nest rimmed with fine, white hair.

After winter, my father pruned the McIntosh the sparrows loved.
Their chittering high up like children playing house in a world of
trees.

In the years of aloneness, my unborn children came diving,
drinking summer's sweet dark under the bridge. I mistook them
for swallows.

Fireweed, bicycle, Alaska. That summer the terns haunted one
curve
in a gravel path. A nest in the rocks and a mother fighting for all
her lives.

September, my son and I bury the limp finch in a shoebox filled
with Black Eyed
Susans. We cradle its head a moment before the darkness comes.

Trade

Every Thursday I dust around the bird's nest
and the eggs we dyed with onion skins
for Easter, blown clean
of their insides and weighing
          barely an ounce. Be careful—

knock them off the mantle
and they shatter into shards
          light as paper.

On the opposite wall, we once hung
a Chagall: a man turned toward
          a bare-breasted woman,
Eiffel Tower in the background, slightly
crooked. But we traded
the Paris love scene for a country road.

I lost a child once. Too early to know
boy or girl.
          Spotting.
The woman's breasts are brush-
          stroked circles, the man reaches

for her. I told my dad he could live with us
          when he's old and wants to die
picking corn or weeding tomatoes.

Oatmeal sticks to his ribs, meat on his bones
and belly, a thin Buddha.

The way he coughs is a memory.
High school band concerts, I'd listen
from the stage, listen
                into the dark,
the shuffling and whispers.
I could pick him out
by the rough leaves in his throat.

The baby we lost
                my son remembers,
                speaks of it in whispers.
The day I got the news,
I called my dad and told him, like a brief
                parenthetical aside,
something you can read or not read.

My friend's doctor gave her a pill
that washes the still baby out
                like yolk:
clean, hollow. The Eiffel Tower dances
behind lovers in a bedroom somewhere—
the outlines of their selves
                as thin as an egg shell.

Fairytale

It's a cottage. The teacups
hold nothing but sun.

The pains are gone
and the child is here.

He sleeps under waves
of breath, smacking

his lips
like the fish

he once was in the lake
of his mother,

now a prince in this
kingdom of air.

Butter on the Bread and Honey on the Butter

There's an engine in the garden
this morning, chugging from yarrow
to cosmos. That beggar of blossoms
carries a dagger, and all his sugar's
the aftermath of spit. Later, the baby's foot
finds him in the grass, and the wailing starts,
high and thin, until we bring
the cut onion to cool it
out of pain. It's a trick: what makes you cry
under the knife
is also a balm. Like each child

I have borne. On the field trip
to the pioneer farm, kids crowd
the kitchen for a chance
to churn butter. The girl in the blue apron
wears her hair in two braids
and upbraids the kids like a mother
for not raising their hands. My son
has just milked a cow, slid
his hands over that strange balloon

that fills with milk slowly
from a place we can't see. He is a room
with one bright window, he was the first
to make honey in my breast.

~~~

The baby roots
the moment he wakes, turning his face
to whatever moves him. Flanked
by his cries, I shift the T–shirt,
everything in the way of the breast
that opens itself like a flower.

~~~

There are days the bee comes sharply
and the sugar hardens
in the dark cupboard. Then I call myself
Honey, take me gently
by the hand. Like bread,

I'm practiced in the art
of rising. Like my son, I'm hungry
for what I don't have.
Jesus called death *the sting*
and we understand. After he raised the dead,
what would they eat, the body
and the spirit fresh with empty?
The good bread of the house
and something on top. They ate their way
back to a consolable hunger,
like a baby, back to that rooting
that loosens the clutch. In the end

of the mouth it's the tongue
searching, the tongue
that finds what's sweet.

My Grandmother Returns to This World

as an evergreen. She stands at the top
of the Crimson Trail breathing quietly
like she always did, Logan River
winding below. The wind doesn't bother
her hair anymore, she doesn't
pat it or adjust her bra
like she used to, but I know her
by the way she faces the world
straight–backed and solid,
one branch holding itself
a little higher. I want to ask her
about the long veils of widows.
She'll just shake her head.

Her sisters surround her as always,
each one a cropping of green
reaching out, surveying
the canyon road cutting its way
into the heart of town
where my grandfather,
now a gnarled scrub oak, was once
a banker, and the woman who will
one day be an aspen
posts a letter in the box
and hears it fall, faintly,
onto some dark floor below.

Like Two People Holding Hands

Someone has hit a cyclist: bicycle wheels suck in
stillness, and black and white cars in tandem read *Police*.
We're going to a wedding
where my husband will stand at the front and officiate,
help the lovers join hands, say
their vows. The deer leap through the trees,
lead us past rows of oaks holding out their arms
toward the two–story chapel: a Pioneer church, a marriage
of brick and stone, staircases north and south, like wings,
and inside wooden pews in two rows for *his* and *hers*.
It's Lane's second marriage and his first serenade
and in the crush of guests Lane's brother smiles
while his wife tells me everything
I missed before this moment: the hole
in Lane's first wife's stomach
big enough to put your fist in, the hole that claimed
her. *She said she was getting better. She said it, but she knew
it wasn't true.* Ten cream cakes from the bakery downtown,
two carrot. When the bride comes in, we all stand up
but no one's sure when to sit down, and the poor cyclist
is lying down somewhere on a gurney hard as a church pew.
After the ceremony Carolyn wants cake but they aren't
cutting it yet so she waits, eats salad instead, tells me
everything I missed before this moment: her mother
returned from a cruise through the Panama Canal. It's funny
the Americas are separated by just that little land bridge,
like two people holding hands. Outside a deer couple
saunters up the street, and the moon above them
is a hole in the sky. If you reach high enough,
you can put your hand through,
find a hand on the other side.

Talking to God Who Smiles Like Buddha

I've carried myself stone-weight
or pebble for a long time now. I get tired sometimes.
We all went away, my brothers and I, but
when we came back, the cows were still there
on the edge of town. They never wanted
to be anything but cows. These nights
when I look up and find me there
where I stood twenty years ago
I'm too ashamed to say much.
I've looked in the world and found
my own life reassembled and given back to me
with broken glass and a birdsong. Sometimes
the lights go out. I just wait.

Acknowledgements

I'm grateful to the publications that first published some of these poems.

All We Can Hold: A Collection of Poetry on Motherhood, "Little Owl in a Dark Room"

Ascent, "Tiger, Hyena Still at Large"

BODY, "At Last the Light in the Trees Wavers" and "My Grandmother Returns to This World"

Clackamas Literary Review, 20th anniversary issue, "The Hidden Honey," "Childhood at Home," and "Passage"

The Cimarron Review, "How His Fingers Trembled"

Crab Orchard Review, "My Son Says He Has an Owl Inside of Him," "Girls of the Underworld," and "Butter on the Bread and Honey on the Butter"

Cutthroat, "The Body Carries Its Own Light"

Gulf Stream, "Autobiography with Birds" and "Concertato"

Juxtaprose, "Trade"

The Poet's Billow, "Fall in a Triptych"

Redactions, "My Possible Pasts"

Rock & Sling, "Nesting Dolls"

Small Orange, "Connie Wolf, the Lady Balloonist From Blue Bell, Pennsylvania, Confesses"

Sugar House Review, "Two Sides of the Same" and "The Spirits Called Legion Speak"

Tar River Poetry, "Envy"

Weber: The Contemporary West, "Wake" and "Acrobats"

"Envy" reprinted in *Tar River Poetry, 30th Anniversary Issue*

"Acrobats" and "Wake" reprinted in *Fire in the Pasture:
    Twenty–First Century Mormon Poets*

Thank you to Laura Stott and Natalie Taylor for their expert
advice, guidance, and friendship. To my professors over the
years: Helen Cannon, Anne Shifrer, Jonathan Johnson, Nance
Van Winckel, and especially Christopher Howell for his
encouragement and understanding. To Diane Goettel and
Angela Leroux-Lindsey for their keen eyes and deep hearts and
for helping me feel so welcome at Black Lawrence Press. To
Kristin Carver for her luminous art that graces the cover, her
energy and enthusiasm. Most of all to my family for their love
and support: Teri Karren for my early intro to poetry and her
own passion for it, David and Kathy Brown, my brothers and
their families, the Wilkinson crew, my extended clan, and my
boys—Cael, Beck and Coop. To Sean, for supporting me in
everything I dream and do. And to my God, the companion of
my life.

Photo: Holli Evans

Sunni Brown Wilkinson's poetry has been published in *Crab Orchard Review*, *Adirondack Review*, *BODY*, *Sugar House Review*, *Cimarron Review*, *Southern Indiana Review* and other journals and anthologies and has been nominated for two Pushcarts. She holds an MFA from the Inland Northwest Center for Writers at Eastern Washington University and teaches at Weber State University. She lives in northern Utah with her husband and three young sons.